Crock Pot Magic

*Delicious Recipes
The Whole Family Will Love!*

Pamela James

Copyright 2014 by: Pamela James

All rights reserved. No part of this book may be reproduced or transmitted to any form by any means electronic or mechanical including photocopying, recording or by any information storage and retrieval system without the written permission of the Publisher except where permitted by law.

Table of Contents

Slow Cooker/Crock Pot Cranberry Pork Loin Roast..4

Crock Pot - Style Loaded Baked Potato Soup..6

BBQ Pulled Pork Sandwiches...8

Ground Beef Stroganoff..10

Mouth Watering Crock Pot Spaghetti Sauce..12

Crock Pot Cream Cheese Chicken...14

Crock Pot Taco Soup..16

Crock Pot Lasagna..18

The Best Chicken Tortilla Soup..20

To Die For Crock Pot Roast...22

Crock-Pot Chicken With Black Beans & Cream Cheese..24

Slow Cooked Chicken, Gravy and Stuffing..26

Auntie's Slow Cooked Vegetarian Chili..28

Cheese Enchilada Chowder..30

Crock Pot Chicken Taco Meat..32

Slow Cooked Whole Chicken...34

Crock Pot Chops That Will Make You Eat Until You Pop!..36

Jambalaya for the Crock Pot...38

Slow-Cooker Beef Short Ribs...40

Slow Cooker Macaroni & Cheese...42

Split Pea Soup (Crock Pot) - Dairy Free..44

Barbecue Country Style Ribs..46

Slow Cooked Thai Chicken Thighs..48

Tasty Barbecue Chicken Sandwiches in the Crock Pot..50

Pasta E Fagioli Soup in a Crock Pot (Olive Garden Style)...52

Delicious Crock Pot Ravioli..54

Crock Pot Chicken Cacciatore..56

Easy Crock Pot Moroccan Chicken, Chickpea and Apricot Tagine...................................58

Savory Cube Steak and Gravy..61

Down Home Crock Pot Chili..63

In Closing..65

Slow Cooker/Crock Pot Cranberry Pork Loin Roast

Prep Time: 20 mins

Total Time: 4 hrs 20 mins

Servings: 6

Ingredients

- 1 (3 -3 1/2 lb) pork loin roast
- 5 tablespoons oil, divided (or use as much as needed)
- 0.5 (1 ounce) package dry onion soup mix
- fresh ground black pepper
- 1 1/2 teaspoons garlic powder
- 8 garlic cloves (optional or use as many as desired, I use lots!)
- 1/3 cup French dressing
- 1 tablespoon cornstarch
- 1 (16 ounce) cans whole berry cranberry sauce

Directions

1. Use a strainer to separate the dried onions from the dry powder; set aside the dry onions in a small bowl.
2. Heat a skillet over medium heat and put 3 tablespoons of oil in it.
3. Rub 2 tablespoons of oil to the pork loin roast, then season the roast with onion soup powder, black pepper and garlic powder.
4. Fry the roast in hot oil until it becomes brown. Let the roast cool until it's easy to handle.
5. Make small slices all over the roast and stuff the roast with garlic cloves. Slice the cloves in half if the cloves are very large. (optional)
6. Put the roast in the slow cooker.
7. Whisk the French dressing and the cornstarch in a bowl. When the mixture becomes smooth, add the cranberry sauce and the dried onions. Mix until all the ingredients are combined.
8. In the slow cooker, pour the mixture on top and around the pork.
9. You may choose on 3 options to cook the pork: on high heat for 4 hours or on low heat for about 7-8 hours or until the pork reaches inner temperature of 160°F.

Nutrition Facts

Serving Size: 1 (336 g)
Servings Per Recipe: 6

Amount Per Serving	% Daily Value
Calories 773.6	
Calories from Fat 356	46%
Total Fat 39.5g	60%
Saturated Fat 10.2g	51%
Cholesterol 183.8mg	61%
Sugars 31.2 g	
Sodium 460.7mg	19%
Total Carbohydrate 36.4g	12%
Dietary Fiber 1.0g	4%
Sugars 31.2 g	125%
Protein 65.7g	131%

Variation:

For more gravy, you may double the cranberry sauce and French dressing. Adjust the cooking time if the roast is larger.

Crock Pot - Style Loaded Baked Potato Soup

Prep Time: 15 mins

Total Time: 5 hrs 15 mins

Serves: 6-8, **Yield:** 2.0 cup servings

Ingredients

- 6 large baking potatoes, peeled, cut in 1/2 -inch cubes
- 1 large onion, chopped
- 1 quart chicken broth
- 3 garlic cloves, minced (or pressed)
- 1/4 cup butter
- 2 1/2 teaspoons salt
- 1 teaspoon pepper
- 1 cup cream or 1 cup half-and-half cream
- 1 cup shredded sharp cheddar cheese
- 3 tablespoons chopped fresh chives
- 1 cup sour cream (optional)
- 8 slices bacon, fried & crumbled
- cheese, for sprinkling

Directions

1. In a large crock pot, gather all the first seven ingredients and combine; cover the pot and cook on HIGH setting for 4 hours or on LOW setting for 8 hours. Be sure that the potatoes should be tender after cooking.
2. Mash the mixture to make the potatoes coarsely chopped. It would also make the soup slightly thickened.
3. Add in the cream, cheese, and chives. Mix it all together but don't over mix it.
4. If you're using sour cream, place it on top. Lastly, sprinkle with bacon and more cheese

Nutrition Facts

Serving Size: 1 (345 g)
Servings Per Recipe: 6

Amount Per Serving	% Daily Value
Calories 478.7	
Calories from Fat 289	60%
Total Fat 32.1g	49%
Saturated Fat 18.4g	92%
Cholesterol 91.5mg	30%
Sugars 3.0 g	
Sodium 1760.9mg	73%
Total Carbohydrate 35.3g	11%
Dietary Fiber 3.2g	13%
Sugars 3.0 g	12%
Protein 13.4g	26%

Variation: Instead of boiling the potatoes, you may bake them. Additional cheese and/or bacon can be added to suit your preferred taste.

BBQ Pulled Pork Sandwiches

Prep Time: 30 mins

Total Time: 10 hrs 30 mins

Servings: 8-10

Ingredients
- 1 1/2-2 lbs pork shoulder
- 1 cup water
- 1 teaspoon dried basil
- 1 teaspoon dried rosemary
- 1 (18 ounce) bottles barbecue sauce

Directions

1. With the water, basil, and rosemary, put the pork shoulder in the crock pot. Cook on low and on high if frozen for about 8 hours. This can be done overnight but be sure to put the heat on low setting even if the pork is frozen.
2. If there's skin or bone, remove it from the pork.
3. By using a fork, draw the meat apart into small pieces. After that, return the meat to the crock pot.
4. Stir in 1 bottle of barbecue sauce and ¼ cup of water to coat the recipe.
5. Cook for 1-2 hours on low setting.
6. Place in hamburger buns, add coleslaw, and serve.

Nutrition Facts

Serving Size: 1 (187 g)
Servings Per Recipe: 6

Amount Per Serving	% Daily Value
Calories 418.6	
Calories from Fat 257	61%
Total Fat 28.5g	43%
Saturated Fat 12.2g	61%
Cholesterol 117.8mg	39%
Sugars 4.0 g	
Sodium 872.1mg	36%
Total Carbohydrate 8.9g	2%
Dietary Fiber 1.2g	5%
Sugars 4.0 g	16%
Protein 30.4g	60%

Variation: Any style of BBQ sauce could be used if you don't prefer the sweet one. Dry sherry may also be added to the water when starting out to add more taste.

Ground Beef Stroganoff

Prep Time: 20 mins

Total Time: 8 hrs 20 mins

Servings: 6-8

Ingredients
- 2 lbs ground beef
- 2 medium onions, chopped
- 2 cloves garlic, minced
- 1 (4 ounce) cans sliced mushrooms, drained
- 1 1/2 teaspoons salt
- 1/4 teaspoon pepper
- 1 cup beef bouillon or 1 cup consommé
- 3 tablespoons tomato paste
- 2 tablespoons flour
- 3/4 cup sour cream, mixed with the flour

Directions

1. In a large skillet, fry the ground beef until brown and add onions, garlic and mushrooms.
2. Sauté until onion is golden brown.
3. Gather the remaining ingredients together with the sautéed meat except for the sour cream and flour and put inside the crock pot.
4. Stir the ingredients completely.
5. Cover the crock pot; cook for 6-8 hours on low setting. You may also cook it in high setting for 3 hours.
6. Take note that the sour cream and flour should be stirred in 1 hour before serving the dish.
7. This can be served over hot buttered noodles or rice.

Nutrition Facts

Serving Size: 1 (187 g)
Servings Per Recipe: 6

Amount Per Serving	% Daily Value
Calories 418.6	
Calories from Fat 257	61%
Total Fat 28.5g	43%
Saturated Fat 12.2g	61%
Cholesterol 117.8mg	39%
Sugars 4.0 g	
Sodium 872.1mg	36%
Total Carbohydrate 8.9g	2%
Dietary Fiber 1.2g	5%
Sugars 4.0 g	16%
Protein 30.4g	60%

Variation: If you like, 1lb of prepackaged Swedish meatballs could be used instead of ground beef. You can also add ¼ tsp nutmeg and 2 tbsp tomato paste to flour and sour cream for more taste.

Mouth Watering Crock Pot Spaghetti Sauce

Prep Time: 20 mins

Total Time: 8 hrs 20 mins

Servings: 12

Ingredients
- 1 lb ground beef
- 1 lb ground pork
- 1 medium onion, chopped fine
- 2 (28 ounce) cans diced tomatoes, with juice
- 2 (6 ounce) cans tomato paste
- 2 (8 ounce) cans tomato sauce
- 2 bay leaves
- 5 garlic cloves, pressed
- 4 teaspoons dried oregano
- 1 1/2 teaspoons salt
- 4 teaspoons dried basil
- 3 tablespoons brown sugar
- 1 teaspoon dried thyme

Directions
    1. Cook the meats and onion in a skillet until brown. After that, drain them well.
    2. From the skillet, transfer the cooked meats and onion to a crock pot.
    3. Include the remaining ingredients in the crock pot and mix thoroughly.
    4. Cover your crock pot and turn the heat to a low setting. Let it cook for 8-10 hours.
    5. Prepare your hot spaghetti noodles and pour mixture on top. Serve.

Nutrition Facts

Serving Size: 1 (289 g)
Servings Per Recipe: 12

Amount Per Serving	% Daily Value
Calories 257.6	
Calories from Fat 127	49%
Total Fat 14.2g	21%
Saturated Fat 5.2g	26%
Cholesterol 52.9mg	17%
Sugars 12.3 g	
Sodium 770.6mg	32%
Total Carbohydrate 17.6g	5%
Dietary Fiber 3.7g	15%
Sugars 12.3 g	49%
Protein 16.6g	33%

Variation: If you're not a fan of ground beef, you may replace it with any kind of meat that would suit your preference.

Crock Pot Cream Cheese Chicken

Prep Time: 20 mins

Total Time: 7 hrs 20 mins

Servings: 6

Ingredients
- 3 lbs chicken pieces
- 1 (2/3 ounce) package Italian salad dressing mix
- 4 tablespoons melted butter (divided)
- 1 small onion, chopped
- 1 garlic clove, chopped
- 1 (10 1/2 ounce) cans cream of chicken soup
- 8 ounces cream cheese
- 1/2 cup chicken broth

Directions
1. First, put the chicken slices into the crock pot. Then drizzle some Italian seasoning over it and add 2 tablespoons of melted butter.
2. Set the heat on low and cook for 4-6 hours.

3. In a sauce pan, melt 2 tablespoons of butter. Sauté onion and garlic in the pan. Combine the cream of chicken soup, cream cheese, and chicken broth inside the pan. Mix until the sauce smoothens.

4. Transfer the mixture to the crock pot and for 1 more hour, cook on low.

Nutrition Facts

Serving Size: 1 (267 g)
Servings Per Recipe: 6

Amount Per Serving	% Daily Value
Calories 547.4	
Calories from Fat 399	73%
Total Fat 44.4g	68%
Saturated Fat 19.0g	95%
Cholesterol 169.4mg	56%
Sugars 2.0 g	
Sodium 696.8mg	29%
Total Carbohydrate 6.4g	2%
Dietary Fiber 0.2g	0%
Sugars 2.0 g	8%
Protein 29.7g	59%

Variation: This dish can be cooked in high setting for 3 ½ hours if you want to save more time. You can add some mushrooms to taste.

Crock Pot Taco Soup

Prep Time: 10 mins

Total Time: 2 hrs 10 mins

Servings: 8-10

Ingredients

- 1 (16 ounce) cans pinto beans
- 1 (16 ounce) cans white beans or 1 (16 ounce) cans kidney beans
- 1 (11 ounce) cans niblet corn
- 1 (11 ounce) cans Rotel tomatoes & chilies
- 1 (28 ounce) cans diced tomatoes
- 1 (4 ounce) cans diced green chilies
- 1 (1 1/4 ounce) envelopes taco seasoning mix
- 1 (1 ounce) envelope Hidden Valley® Original Ranch® Dressing and Seasoning Mix
- 1 lb shredded chicken, ground beef or 1 lb any meat

Directions

1. Cook shredded chicken, ground beef or any meat of your choice. After cooking, drain.
2. If needed, you may shred the meat.
3. Prepare your crock pot and add all the ingredients in it.

4. Remember not to drain cans.
5. Stir the mixture in the crock pot.
6. You may cook this dish on high setting for 2 hours or on low setting for 4 hours.
7. Set the heat on low until serving to keep the dish hot.
8. Dress your dish with sour cream, shredded cheese, chopped green onions, or tortilla chips.

Nutrition Facts

Serving Size: 1 (292 g)
Servings Per Recipe: 8

Amount Per Serving	% Daily Value
Calories 339.2	
Calories from Fat 89	26%
Total Fat 9.9g	15%
Saturated Fat 2.6g	13%
Cholesterol 42.5mg	14%
Sugars 6.0 g	
Sodium 729.6mg	30%
Total Carbohydrate 43.4g	14%
Dietary Fiber 10.9g	43%
Sugars 6.0 g	24%
Protein 22.3g	44%

Variation: ½ cup of rice may also be added but you would need to cook it on low setting for about 6 hours.

Crock Pot Lasagna

Prep Time: 15 mins

Total Time: 4 hrs 15 mins

Servings: 4-6

Ingredients
- 1 lb lean ground beef
- 1 onion, chopped
- 2 garlic cloves, smashed
- 1 (28 ounce) cans tomato sauce
- 1 (6 ounce) cans tomato paste
- 1 1/2 teaspoons salt
- 1 teaspoon dried oregano
- 12 ounces cottage cheese (we like 2%)
- 1/2 cup grated parmesan cheese or 1/2 cup asiago cheese
- 12 ounces lasagna noodles, uncooked
- 16 ounces shredded mozzarella cheese

Directions
1. In a frying pan, cook ground beef, onion, and garlic until brown.
2. Include tomato sauce, tomato paste, salt, and oregano in the pan.

3. Cook the mixture until warm.
4. In the slow cooker, form a layer of meat sauce in the bottom.
5. Place a double layer of uncooked lasagna noodles. Break the noodles so that it can fit the slow cooker. Top with cheeses.
6. Repeat the process of putting sauce, noodles, and cheeses until all are already inside the slow cooker.
7. Set the heat to low; cover and cook for about 4 to 5 hours.

Nutrition Facts

Serving Size: 1 (460 g)
Servings Per Recipe: 4

Amount Per Serving		% Daily Value
Calories 1098.2		
Calories from Fat 415		37%
Total Fat	46.1g	70%
Saturated Fat	23.6g	118%
Cholesterol	190.0mg	63%
Sugars	20.9 g	
Sodium	3576.5mg	149%
Total Carbohydrate	92.0g	30%
Dietary Fiber	8.1g	32%
Sugars	20.9 g	83%
Protein	78.9g	157%

Variation: To sweeten the tomato mixture, 2 tablespoons of sugar may be added.

The Best Chicken Tortilla Soup

Prep Time: 15 mins

Total Time: 6 hrs 15 mins

Servings: 6

Ingredients
- 1 (46 ounce) cans chicken broth
- 1 (15 ounce) cans tomato sauce
- 1 (15 ounce) cans diced tomatoes
- 3 cups cooked chicken, shredded (I use rotisserie from the deli)
- 2 Anaheim chilies, diced
- 1 jalapeno pepper, diced
- 1/2 cup diced onion
- 3 -4 large tomatoes, diced
- 2 garlic cloves, minced
- 2 tablespoons minced cilantro
- 1 tablespoon chili powder
- 2 teaspoons cumin
- 2 teaspoons pepper
- 1 teaspoon salt
- 2 teaspoons Tabasco sauce (I use the chipotle flavor)

- 1/2 teaspoon chipotle pepper (optional)

Garnish
- 1 cup shredded cheddar cheese
- 1 avocado, chopped
- 1/4 cup cilantro, pulled from stem
- 1 lime, cut into wedges
- 2 cups crushed tortilla chips

Directions

1. Place all of the ingredients except for the garnishes in the crock pot. Set the heat on high and cook for 5-6 hours.
2. Dress the dish with garnishes and it's a must to squeeze lime in it.
3. Serve dish.
4. You can still do this even if you're not using a crock pot. First, heat 2 tablespoons of olive oil and sauté the garlic and onion. After that, add the remaining ingredients.
5. Let the dish boil in low temperature for at least an hour so that the flavors would mix together

Nutrition Facts

Serving Size: 1 (647 g)
Servings Per Recipe: 6

Amount Per Serving	% Daily Value
Calories 398.0	
Calories from Fat 180	45%
Total Fat 20.0g	30%
Saturated Fat 6.7g	33%
Cholesterol 72.2mg	24%
Sugars 10.1 g	
Sodium 1729.4mg	72%
Total Carbohydrate 25.6g	8%
Dietary Fiber 7.3g	29%
Sugars 10.1 g	40%
Protein 31.6g	63%

Variation: For a different touch, 1 can of red enchilada sauce may replace the tomato sauce.

To Die For Crock Pot Roast

Prep Time: 5 mins

Total Time: 9 hrs 5 mins

Servings: 8

Ingredients
- 1 (4 -5 lb) beef roast, any kind
- 1 (1 1/4 ounce) packages brown gravy mix, dry
- 1 (1 1/4 ounce) packages dried Italian salad dressing mix
- 1 (1 1/4 ounce) packages ranch dressing mix, dry
- 1/2 cup water

Directions
1. Prepare beef roast inside the crock pot.
2. In a bowl, mix all the dried mixes together. After mixing, sprinkle on top of the roast.
3. Pour water around the roast.
4. Cover and cook for 7-9 hours on low heat.

Nutrition Facts

Serving Size: 1 (245 g)
Servings Per Recipe: 8

Amount Per Serving		% Daily Value
Calories 295.2		
Calories from Fat 87		29%
Total Fat 9.7g		14%
Saturated Fat 3.9g		19%
Cholesterol 149.8mg		49%
Sugars 0.0 g		
Sodium 380.5mg		15%
Total Carbohydrate 2.6g		0%
Dietary Fiber 0.0g		0%
Sugars 0.0 g		0%
Protein 49.5g		99%

Variation: A 3 lb boneless chuck roast can be used. Divide the ranch dressing in half and add ¼ cup of water. The dish will still cook for 9 hours.

Crock-Pot Chicken With Black Beans & Cream Cheese

Prep Time: 3 mins

Total Time: 4 hrs 3 mins

Ingredients

- 4 -5 boneless chicken breasts
- 1 (15 1/2 ounce) cans black beans
- 1 (15 ounce) cans corn
- 1 (15 ounce) jars salsa, any kind
- 1 (8 ounce) packages cream cheese

Directions

1. Place 4-5 frozen boneless chicken breasts into your crock pot.
2. Drain the black beans, and the corn. Add it together with the salsa.
3. Set the heat on high for about 4-5 hours or until chicken is cooked.
4. Pour in 1 package of cream cheese and set aside for ½ hour.
5. Serve the dish.

Nutrition Facts

Serving Size: 1 (493 g)
Servings Per Recipe: 4

Amount Per Serving	% Daily Value
Calories 679.1	
Calories from Fat 315	46%

Amount Per Serving	% Daily Value
Total Fat 35.0g	53%
Saturated Fat 15.1g	75%
Cholesterol 155.2mg	51%
Sugars 9.9 g	
Sodium 913.4mg	38%
Total Carbohydrate 50.0g	16%
Dietary Fiber 11.1g	44%
Sugars 9.9 g	39%
Protein 45.8g	91%

Variation: Thawing the chicken can also be done before cooking. Just pay attention as the dish cooks since the cooking time would be shorter. Diced onion, diced green pepper, and jarred jalapenos are also a good addition for extra flavors.

Slow Cooked Chicken, Gravy and Stuffing

Prep Time: 20 mins

Total Time: 6 hrs 20 mins

Servings: 4

<u>Ingredients</u>
- 4 boneless skinless chicken breasts
- salt
- pepper
- 1 cup chicken broth
- 4 -6 slices swiss cheese
- 1 (10 1/2 ounce) cans cream of chicken soup
- 1 (10 1/2 ounce) cans cream of mushroom soup
- 1/4 cup milk
- 2 cups Pepperidge Farm Herb Stuffing
- 1/2 cup butter, Melted

Directions

1. Add salt and pepper to chicken breasts to taste. Place it in crock pot and pour chicken broth in it.
2. On each breast, place a slice of Swiss cheese. Before pouring in the crock pot, the soup and milk should be combined.
3. Pour the soup mixture in. After that, sprinkle the stuffing mix.
4. Add the melted butter on top.
5. This may be cooked in low heat for 6 hours or in high heat for 3 hours.

Nutrition Facts

Serving Size: 1 (399 g)
Servings Per Recipe: 4

Amount Per Serving	% Daily Value
Calories 594.1	
Calories from Fat 390	65%

Amount Per Serving	% Daily Value
Total Fat 43.4g	66%
Saturated Fat 22.9g	114%
Cholesterol 170.3mg	56%
Sugars 2.0 g	
Sodium 1632.2mg	68%
Total Carbohydrate 12.7g	4%
Dietary Fiber 0.0g	0%
Sugars 2.0 g	8%
Protein 37.5g	75%

Variation: For a boost of flavor to the dish, adding garlic powder along with the salt and pepper on the sides of the chicken.

Auntie's Slow Cooked Vegetarian Chili

Prep Time: 15 mins

Total Time: 6 hrs 15 mins

Servings: 8

Ingredients
- 1 (11 ounce) cans condensed black bean soup (or canned black beans in juice)
- 1 (15 ounce) cans kidney beans, drained and rinsed
- 1 (15 ounce) cans garbanzo beans, drained and rinsed (sometimes I use lentils)
- 1 (16 ounce) cans vegetarian baked beans
- 1 (14 1/2 ounce) cans chopped tomato puree (I use large 29 oz. can crushed tomatoes)
- 1 (15 ounce) cans whole kernel corn, drained
- 1 onion, chopped
- 1 green bell pepper, chopped

- 2 zucchini, chopped
- 2 stalks celery, chopped
- 2 garlic cloves, chopped
- 1 (4 ounce) cans diced chilies
- 1 -2 jalapeno, chopped (depending on how much heat you want)
- 1 tablespoon chili powder
- 2 teaspoons cumin
- 1 tablespoon dried parsley
- 1 tablespoon dried oregano
- 1 tablespoon dried basil
- 1 tablespoon cilantro (optional)

Directions
1. Sauté the onion, bell pepper, zucchini, and celery for 5 minutes in a sauce pan.
2. The black bean soup, kidney beans, garbanzo beans, baked beans, tomatoes, corn, onion, bell pepper, zucchini, jalapeno, chilies, and celery must be combined in the slow cooker.
3. Add the garlic, chili powder, cumin, parsley, oregano, and basil (cilantro is optional to add)
4. On low setting, cook for about 6 hours.
5. May be served with tortillas, cornbread, rice, or French bread.
6. Enjoy!
7. This can be frozen for future use.
8. If there are any leftovers, it can also be a good topping for nachos.

Nutrition Facts

Serving Size: 1 (415 g)
Servings Per Recipe: 8

Amount Per Serving	% Daily Value
Calories 293.7	
Calories from Fat 25	76%
Total Fat 2.8g	4%
Saturated Fat 0.5g	2%
Cholesterol 0.0mg	0%
Sugars 13.5 g	
Sodium 1114.8mg	46%
Total Carbohydrate 59.3g	19%
Dietary Fiber 14.3g	57%
Sugars 13.5 g	54%
Protein 13.9g	27%

Variation: A can of spicy chili beans can substitute baked beans.

Cheese Enchilada Chowder

Prep Time: 25 mins

Total Time: 6 hrs 25 mins

Servings: 6

Ingredients
- 1 (15 ounce) cans black beans, rinsed and drained
- 1 (14 1/2 ounce) cans diced tomatoes, drained
- 1 (10 ounce) packages frozen whole kernel corn
- 1/2 cup chopped onion
- 1/2 cup chopped yellow bell peppers or 1/2 cup red bell peppers or 1/2 cup green bell pepper
- 1 jalapeno pepper, seeded, and finely chopped
- 1 (19 ounce) cans enchilada sauce
- 1 (10 3/4 ounce) cans cream of chicken soup
- 2 cups milk

- 1 cup shredded monterey jack cheese
- 1 cup shredded cheddar cheese
- sour cream
- guacamole
- tortilla chips

Directions

1. Combine the black beans, tomatoes, frozen corn, onion, bell pepper, and jalapeno pepper in a 4 quart slow cooker. Stir the mixture together.

2. Whisk the enchilada sauce and cream soup in a mixing bowl.

3. Slowly, add the milk and whisk until smooth.

4. Add the vegetable in the slow cooker.

5. Cover the slow cooker. For 6-8 hours, cook the dish on low heat.

6. Sprinkle the cheese over. Stir until the cheese melts.

7. Pour hot soup into serving bowls. Sour cream, guacamole, and broken tortilla chips may be optional toppings.

Nutrition Facts

Serving Size: 1 (459 g)
Servings Per Recipe: 6

Amount Per Serving	% Daily Value
Calories 414.9	
Calories from Fat 168	40%
Total Fat 18.7g	28%
Saturated Fat 10.4g	52%
Cholesterol 51.9mg	17%
Sugars 8.9 g	
Sodium 1399.0mg	58%
Total Carbohydrate 43.0g	14%
Dietary Fiber 8.4g	33%
Sugars 8.9 g	35%
Protein 21.6g	43%

Variation: Instead of cream of chicken, you may also use vegetable cream soup to go in the dish.

Crock Pot Chicken Taco Meat

Prep Time: 0 mins

Total Time: 6 hrs

Servings: 8

Ingredients
- 3 tablespoons taco seasoning,
- 1 cup chicken broth
- 1 lb boneless skinless chicken breast

Directions
1. Prepare chicken broth and pour taco seasoning. Mix until seasoning is dissolved.
2. Put the chicken breast first in the crock pot before pouring the chicken broth in.
3. Cover your crock pot and then let it cook for 6-8 hours on low setting.
4. Shred the chicken into bite-sized pieces by using two forks.
5. Freeze the dish by placing the meat with the juices into freezer bags.
6. Remember to press all the air out before sealing the freezer bags.

Nutrition Facts

Serving Size: 1 (88 g)
Servings Per Recipe: 8

Amount Per Serving	% Daily Value
Calories 71.4	
Calories from Fat 14	20%

Amount Per Serving		% Daily Value
Total Fat 1.6g		2%
Saturated Fat 0.3g		1%
Cholesterol 36.3mg		12%
Sugars 0.2 g		
Sodium 239.3mg		9%
Total Carbohydrate 0.6g		0%
Dietary Fiber 0.1g		0%
Sugars 0.2 g		1%
Protein 12.6g		25%

Variation: You may also add minced garlic and cayenne pepper before serving with soft tortillas, soft tacos, and hard shells.

Slow Cooked Whole Chicken

Prep Time: 15 hrs

Total Time: 23 hrs

Servings: 4

Ingredients

- 4 teaspoons salt (per recipe reviews, 2 tsp is better)
- 2 teaspoons paprika
- 1 teaspoon cayenne pepper
- 1 teaspoon onion powder
- 1 teaspoon thyme
- 1 teaspoon white pepper
- 1/2 teaspoon garlic powder
- 1/2 teaspoon black pepper
- 1 large roasting chicken (with pop-up timer if possible)
- 1 cup chopped onion (optional)

Directions

1. Mix all the spices in a small bowl.
2. Clean the chicken and remove as well any giblets you may see.
3. Rub the chicken with the spice mixture.

4. Put the chicken in a re-sealable plastic bag and refrigerate overnight. You may skip this if you're in a hurry.
5. Before cooking the dish, place the chopped onion at the bottom of the crock pot.
6. Put the chicken in. You won't be needing any liquid since the juices will come out of the chicken.
7. Let it cook on low heat for 4-8 hours.
8. Tip: A pop-up timer in the chicken can be helpful because some crock pots may cook the chicken faster/slower than the others.

Nutrition Facts

Serving Size: 1 (196 g)
Servings Per Recipe: 4

Amount Per Serving	% Daily Value
Calories 327.0	
Calories from Fat 211	64%

Amount Per Serving	% Daily Value
Total Fat 23.4g	36%
Saturated Fat 6.6g	33%
Cholesterol 106.9mg	35%
Sugars 0.2 g	
Sodium 2426.7mg	101%
Total Carbohydrate 2.2g	0%
Dietary Fiber 0.8g	3%
Sugars 0.2 g	0%
Protein 25.5g	51%

Variation: If you want to reduce the cooking time to 4 ½ hours, bone-in chicken breasts can be used instead of a whole chicken.

Crock Pot Chops That Will Make You Eat Until You Pop!

Prep Time: 10 mins

Total Time: 6 hrs 10 mins

Servings: 4

Ingredients
- 4 pork chops, each about 1/2 inch thick
- 2 medium onions, chopped
- 2 celery ribs, chopped
- 1 large green pepper, sliced
- 1 (14 1/2 ounce) cans stewed tomatoes
- 1/2 cup ketchup
- 2 tablespoons cider vinegar
- 2 tablespoons brown sugar
- 2 tablespoons Worcestershire sauce
- 1 tablespoon lemon juice
- 1 beef bouillon cube
- 2 tablespoons cornstarch
- 2 tablespoons water

Directions

1. Season pork chops with salt and pepper if desired.
2. Set aside the water and cornstarch. Add the remaining ingredients to the crock pot.
3. On low heat setting, cook for 5 ½ hours.
4. In a small bowl, mix the cornstarch and water. After mixing, pour it into the crock pot.
5. Add 30 minutes more to the cooking time.
6. Place dish over rice and serve.

Nutrition Facts

Serving Size: 1 (495 g)
Servings Per Recipe: 4

Amount Per Serving	% Daily Value
Calories 483.7	
Calories from Fat 167	34%
Total Fat 18.5g	28%
Saturated Fat 6.1g	30%
Cholesterol 137.4mg	45%
Sugars 22.3 g	
Sodium 1049.1mg	43%
Total Carbohydrate 34.8g	11%
Dietary Fiber 3.2g	12%
Sugars 22.3 g	89%
Protein 44.1g	88%

Variation: Spiral noodles may also be used instead of rice and you may cut the pork chops into bite sized cubes.

Jambalaya for the Crock Pot

Prep Time: 10 mins

Total Time: 8 hrs 10 mins

Servings: 6

Ingredients

- 12 ounces boneless skinless chicken breasts
- 1 1/2 cups green peppers, chopped
- 1 medium onion, chopped
- 2 celery ribs, sliced
- 4 garlic cloves, minced
- 1 (14 ounce) cans whole tomatoes
- 1/3 cup tomato paste
- 1 (10 1/2 ounce) cans beef broth
- 1 tablespoon parsley
- 1 1/2 teaspoons basil
- 1/2 teaspoon oregano
- 1 teaspoon Tabasco sauce

- 1/2 teaspoon cayenne pepper
- 1/2 teaspoon salt
- 1 lb shrimp, shelled
- 3 cups cooked rice

Directions

1. Slice the chicken into pieces measuring at about 1 inch.
2. Except for the shrimp and rice, place all the ingredients into the crock pot.
3. Cover the dish and cook for 8 hours in low heat.
4. In the last 20 minutes of cooking, add the shrimp.
5. Before serving, you may stir in the rice.

Nutrition Facts

Serving Size: 1 (434 g)
Servings Per Recipe: 6

Amount Per Serving		% Daily Value
Calories 288.2		
Calories from Fat 26		53%
Total Fat 2.9g		4%
Saturated Fat 0.5g		2%
Cholesterol 131.5mg		43%
Sugars 5.6 g		
Sodium 1008.6mg		42%
Total Carbohydrate 37.4g		12%
Dietary Fiber 3.0g		12%
Sugars 5.6 g		22%
Protein 27.1g		54%

Variation: For a spicier version: You will need 2 chicken breasts, 3 turkey sausages & 1 lb of shrimp. Add 1 can of diced spicy tomatoes, seasoned with jalapeño and a small can of garlic roasted tomato paste. Leave out the salt, but add 1 teaspoon of Cajun seasoning & triple the Tabasco sauce.

Slow-Cooker Beef Short Ribs

Prep Time: 10 mins

Total Time: 9 hrs 10 mins

Servings: 6

Ingredients
- 1/3 cup flour
- 1 teaspoon salt
- 1/4 teaspoon pepper
- 2 1/2 lbs boneless beef short ribs
- 1/4 cup butter
- 1 cup chopped onion
- 1 cup beef broth
- 3/4 cup red wine vinegar
- 3/4 cup brown sugar
- 1/4 cup chili sauce
- 2 tablespoons catsup
- 2 tablespoons Worcestershire sauce

- 2 tablespoons minced garlic
- 1 teaspoon chili powder

Directions
1. Inside a plastic bag, put flour, salt, and pepper.
2. Insert the ribs in the bag. Shake to coat the ribs with the seasoning and flour.
3. Remove the ribs in the bag. In a large skillet, fry the ribs until brown.
4. When the ribs are already brown, transfer it in the slow cooker.
5. Combine remaining ingredients in the same skillet used to brown the ribs.
6. Stir and bring the mixture to a boil.
7. Remove the mixture in the skillet and pour it over the ribs.
8. Cover your slow cooker and set the heat on low. Allow the dish to cook for 9 hours.

Nutrition Facts

Serving Size: 1 (356 g)
Servings Per Recipe: 6

Amount Per Serving	% Daily Value
Calories 976.7	
Calories from Fat 688	70%
Total Fat 76.4g	117%
Saturated Fat 34.7g	173%
Cholesterol 163.9mg	54%
Sugars 30.8 g	
Sodium 979.1mg	40%
Total Carbohydrate 40.6g	13%
Dietary Fiber 1.5g	6%
Sugars 30.8 g	123%
Protein 29.4g	58%

Variation: For a shorter cooking time, you may cook the dish on high setting for 4 hours and for 1 ½ hours continue to cook on low heat.

Slow Cooker Macaroni & Cheese

Prep Time: 5 mins

Total Time: 3 hrs 5 mins

Servings: 12

Ingredients
- 2 cups uncooked elbow macaroni
- 4 tablespoons butter, cut into pieces
- 2 1/2 cups grated sharp cheddar cheese or 10 ounces sharp cheddar cheese
- 3 eggs, beaten
- 1/2 cup sour cream
- 1 (10 3/4 ounce) cans condensed cheddar cheese soup

- 1/2 teaspoon salt
- 1 cup whole milk
- 1/2 teaspoon dry mustard
- 1/2 teaspoon black pepper

Directions

1. Prepare a 2 quart sauce pan with lots of water and boil the macaroni for 7 minutes. After that, drain the water to separate macaroni.
2. Mix butter and cheese in a medium saucepan. Keep on stirring the mixture until the cheese melts.
3. Stir the cheese/butter mixture, eggs, sour cream, soup, salt, milk, mustard, and pepper in a slow cooker.
4. Get your drained macaroni and continue stirring.
5. Allow it to cook for 3 hours with occasional stirring.

Nutrition Facts

Serving Size: 1 (114 g)
Servings Per Recipe: 12

Amount Per Serving	% Daily Value
Calories 273.9	
Calories from Fat 159	58%
Total Fat 17.7g	27%
Saturated Fat 10.6g	53%
Cholesterol 94.2mg	31%
Sugars 2.1 g	
Sodium 488.1mg	20%
Total Carbohydrate 16.8g	5%
Dietary Fiber 0.8g	3%
Sugars 2.1 g	8%
Protein 11.7g	23%

Variation: Increase this dish's smoothness by using gouda cheese to go with the cheddar cheese and substitute milk with cream.

Split Pea Soup (Crock Pot) - Dairy Free

Prep Time: 10 mins

Total Time: 6 hrs 10 mins

Servings: 4-6

Ingredients
- 1 (16 ounce) packages dried split peas, rinsed
- 2 cups diced ham
- 3 carrots, peeled and sliced
- 1 medium onion, chopped
- 2 stalks celery, plus leaves, chopped
- 2 garlic cloves, minced
- 1 bay leaf
- 1/2 tablespoon seasoning salt
- 1/2 teaspoon fresh pepper
- 1 1/2 quarts hot water or 1 1/2 quarts broth

Directions

1. Place the ingredients in the crock pot.
2. Flow in the water but don't stir yet.
3. Cover crock pot. You may cook this using 2 methods: on high for 4-5 hours or on low for 8-10 hours.
4. Take the bay leaf out.
5. This can be served with a crispy bread or bun.

Nutrition Facts

Serving Size: 1 (422 g)
Servings Per Recipe: 4

Amount Per Serving	% Daily Value
Calories 525.5	
Calories from Fat 49	41%
Total Fat 5.5g	8%
Saturated Fat 1.5g	7%
Cholesterol 36.4mg	12%
Sugars 12.7 g	
Sodium 1137.8mg	47%
Total Carbohydrate 76.7g	25%
Dietary Fiber 31.1g	124%
Sugars 12.7 g	51%
Protein 44.4g	88%

Variation: For a thinner soup, 2 quarts of water would do the trick.

Barbecue Country Style Ribs

Prep Time: 10 mins

Total Time: 6 hrs 10 mins

Servings: 4-6

Ingredients
- 4 -5 lbs country-style pork ribs
- 1 (18 ounce) bottles of your favorite barbecue sauce
- 1 onion, chopped
- salt and pepper, to taste

Directions
1. Throw in all the ingredients in crock pot.
2. Set the heat on low and this this would cook for about 6-8 hours.
3. Be careful in removing from the crock pot since the meat will be falling off the bones. Especially the small ones.

Nutrition Facts

Serving Size: 1 (415 g)
Servings Per Recipe: 4

Amount Per Serving	% Daily Value
Calories 1080.7	
Calories from Fat 487	45%

Amount Per Serving	% Daily Value
Total Fat 54.1g	83%
Saturated Fat 10.7g	53%
Cholesterol 336.2mg	112%
Sugars 37.8 g	
Sodium 1478.4mg	61%
Total Carbohydrate 53.5g	17%
Dietary Fiber 1.3g	5%
Sugars 37.8 g	151%
Protein 88.1g	176%

Variation: A different flavor of BBQ sauce can also be used. The ribs may be boneless or bone-in.

Slow Cooked Thai Chicken Thighs

Prep Time: 5 mins

Total Time: 6 hrs 5 mins

Servings: 4

Ingredients
- 8 boneless, skinless chicken thighs
- 1 (16 ounce) jars cilantro salsa (or any salsa you prefer)
- 1/2 cup peanut butter (crunchy or creamy)
- 2 teaspoons ginger
- 2 tablespoons soy sauce
- 2 teaspoons lime juice

Directions
1. In a crock pot, cook all ingredients with low heat for 6-8 hours.
2. Flavor with cilantro, scallions, and peanuts.
3. Serve dish with Jasmine rice. Rice should be made with 1 cup raw rice, 1 cup water, and 1 cup coconut milk.

Nutrition Facts

Serving Size: 1 (182 g)
Servings Per Recipe: 4

Amount Per Serving	% Daily Value
Calories 362.9	
Calories from Fat 195	53%

Amount Per Serving	% Daily Value
Total Fat 21.7g	33%
Saturated Fat 4.7g	23%
Cholesterol 114.5mg	38%
Sugars 3.2 g	
Sodium 769.7mg	32%
Total Carbohydrate 7.6g	2%
Dietary Fiber 2.1g	8%
Sugars 3.2 g	12%
Protein 36.2g	72%

Variations: Make this spicier by adding Sriracha sauce to taste. Fresh cilantro is also a good choice to add.

Tasty Barbecue Chicken Sandwiches in the Crock Pot

Prep Time: 10 mins

Total Time: 8 hrs 10 mins

Servings: 4-6

Ingredients
- 1 -2 lb boneless skinless chicken breast
- 1 (18 ounce) jars of your favorite barbecue sauce
- 1 medium sweet onion, sliced
- 4 -6 hamburger buns

Directions
1. Before putting the chicken in the crock pot. Eliminate all the visible fat first.
2. Top the chicken with the onion cuts.
3. Add the BBQ sauce all over the chicken and onion.
4. It's not necessary to empty the whole jar. Estimate what's sufficient to spread over the whole chicken.
5. On low heat setting, cook the chicken on an estimated time of 8 hours or just enough to make the chicken tender.

6. Use a fork and knife to shred the chicken to strips. Take some of the mixture and spread onto the top and bottom buns.
7. Leaving the buns out is also an option. The chicken breasts could be eaten as is.
8. Serve it the way you like it.
9. This dish would surely keep your kitchen from heating up in the summertime.
10. Can also be served alongside potato chips and some carrot and raisin salad.

Nutrition Facts

Serving Size: 1 (216 g)
Servings Per Recipe: 4

Amount Per Serving	% Daily Value
Calories 471.3	
Calories from Fat 47	10%
Total Fat 5.2g	8%
Saturated Fat 1.1g	5%
Cholesterol 72.6mg	24%
Sugars 40.5 g	
Sodium 1529.8mg	63%
Total Carbohydrate 74.8g	24%
Dietary Fiber 2.2g	8%
Sugars 40.5 g	162%
Protein 28.4g	56%

Variation: To increase the juiciness of the chicken, tear the chicken at around 4 ½ hours of cooking time and pour on some Sweet Baby Ray's barbeque sauce. Include some liquid smoke in it as well.

Pasta E Fagioli Soup in a Crock Pot (Olive Garden Style)

Prep Time: 15 mins

Total Time: 7 hrs 15 mins

Servings: 12-14

Ingredients

- 2 lbs ground beef
- 1 onion, chopped
- 3 carrots, chopped
- 4 stalks celery, chopped
- 2 (28 ounce) cans diced tomatoes, undrained
- 1 (16 ounce) cans red kidney beans, drained
- 1 (16 ounce) cans white kidney beans, drained
- 3 (10 ounce) cans beef stock
- 3 teaspoons oregano
- 2 teaspoons pepper
- 5 teaspoons parsley
- 1 teaspoon Tabasco sauce (optional)

- 1 (20 ounce) jars spaghetti sauce
- 8 ounces pasta

Directions

1. Heat your skillet and cook the beef until brown.
2. Using a strainer, drain fat from beef before transferring to crock pot. Add all the ingredients in except for the pasta.
3. Choose from two ways to cook it: on low for 7-8 hours or on high for 4-5 hours.
4. At the last 30 minutes on high or at the last 1 hour on low, throw in the pasta.

Nutrition Facts

Serving Size: 1 (375 g)
Servings Per Recipe: 12

Amount Per Serving	% Daily Value
Calories 377.2	
Calories from Fat 119	31%
Total Fat 13.2g	20%
Saturated Fat 4.8g	24%
Cholesterol 51.9mg	17%
Sugars 8.4 g	
Sodium 560.8mg	23%
Total Carbohydrate 40.0g	13%
Dietary Fiber 8.6g	34%
Sugars 8.4 g	33%
Protein 24.6g	49%

Variation: Less or more water can change the soup's consistency.

Delicious Crock Pot Ravioli

Prep Time: 10 mins

Total Time: 4 hrs 10 mins

Servings: 6-8

Ingredients
- 1 (25 ounce) bags beef ravioli
- 1 (26 ounce) jars pasta sauce
- 1 (8 ounce) cans tomato sauce
- 1 cup water
- 2 -3 teaspoons red peppers
- Italian spices
- 1 cup shredded mozzarella cheese

Directions

1. Measure half of the pasta sauce and put it at the bottom of the crock pot.
2. After pouring the pasta sauce, place the frozen ravioli in.
3. When the ravioli is already placed in the crock pot, pour the rest of the pasta sauce. Add the tomato sauce, water, and red pepper as well. Be sure to place it on top of the ravioli. Mixing the tomato sauce, water, and red pepper in the empty pasta sauce jar is also a great idea before adding it in.
4. Italian seasonings should be topped over the sauces.
5. Top it all off with cheese.
6. Set the crock pot to low heat and let it cook for 4-5 hours or until the ravioli gets tender.

Nutrition Facts

Serving Size: 1 (189 g)
Servings Per Recipe: 6

Amount Per Serving	% Daily Value
Calories 186.5	
Calories from Fat 71	38%
Total Fat 7.9g	12%
Saturated Fat 3.4g	17%
Cholesterol 17.5mg	5%
Sugars 14.1 g	
Sodium 888.6mg	37%
Total Carbohydrate 21.6g	7%
Dietary Fiber 4.2g	16%
Sugars 14.1 g	56%
Protein 7.1g	14%

Variation: If you're not a fan of beef, different variants of ravioli may be used.

Crock Pot Chicken Cacciatore

Prep Time: 5 mins

Total Time: 9 hrs 5 mins

Servings: 4

Ingredients
- 3 lbs chicken, cut up in pieces
- 1 large onion, thinly sliced
- 2 (6 ounce) cans tomato paste
- 6 ounces sliced mushrooms
- 1 green bell pepper, finely chopped
- 2 -4 garlic cloves, minced
- 2 teaspoons oregano
- 1 teaspoon dried basil
- 1/2 teaspoon celery powder
- 1 teaspoon salt
- 1/2 cup dry white wine
- 3 tablespoons olive oil

• 1 teaspoon crushed red pepper flakes (optional)

Directions
1. Layer the onions at the bottom of the crock pot.
2. Place the chicken pieces.
3. Add all the other ingredients with the chicken pieces. Stir.
4. Remember to pour the ingredients over chicken while stirring.
5. Cooking this dish on low heat may take 7-9 hours, but on high heat, it will take 3-4 hours.
6. There are two ways to serve this dish. That's serving it over pasta or rice.

Nutrition Facts

Serving Size: 1 (579 g)
Servings Per Recipe: 4

Amount Per Serving	% Daily Value
Calories 948.7	
Calories from Fat 558	58%
Total Fat 62.0g	95%
Saturated Fat 16.2g	81%
Cholesterol 255.1mg	85%
Sugars 13.8 g	
Sodium 1503.2mg	62%
Total Carbohydrate 23.9g	7%
Dietary Fiber 5.2g	21%
Sugars 13.8 g	55%
Protein 69.1g	138%

Variation: To the garlic fanatics, garlic can be added to this dish and you may add as much as you want. Boneless, skinless chicken is also a great choice.

Easy Crock Pot Moroccan Chicken, Chickpea and Apricot Tagine

Prep Time: 30 mins

Total Time: 3 hrs 30 mins

Servings: 6

Ingredients

- 6 large boneless, skinless chicken breasts, chopped into large chunks (or assorted chicken pieces, about 3 lbs)
- 1 tablespoon flour or 2 tablespoons corn flour
- 2 large onions, chopped
- 3 -4 garlic cloves, chopped finely
- 1 -2 tablespoon extra virgin olive oil
- 1 inch fresh gingerroot, finely chopped
- 6 ounces dried apricots
- 2 tablespoons tomato paste
- 2 (14 ounce) cans chopped tomatoes
- 2 (14 ounce) cans chickpeas

- 3 tablespoons honey
- 1/2 pint chicken stock
- 1 pinch saffron or 1 teaspoon turmeric
- 4 teaspoons ras el hanout spice mix (or make up spice mix below)
- 1 teaspoon ground coriander
- 1 teaspoon ground cinnamon
- 1 teaspoon ground cumin
- 1 teaspoon cayenne pepper (optional)
- salt and black pepper
- chopped fresh coriander, to serve (Cilantro)

OPTIONAL
- 2 carrots, peeled & diced (optional)
- 1 preserved lemon, chopped into small wedges (optional)

Directions

1. Just a reminder; if you'll use dried chickpeas, soak and cook them first.
2. Allow 5-10 minutes to sauté chopped onions and garlic in olive oil by using a frying pan or skillet.
3. Pour in the chicken stock. Bit by bit add the flour or corn flour in . Mix until the lumps disappear.
4. Together with the salt and pepper, throw in the herbs, spices, and finely chopped ginger.
5. Open the canned tomatoes and add it to the dish. Mix well.
6. Transfer the tomato, onion, and spice mixture into a slow cooker or tagine.
7. Place the chicken in. Add the chickpeas as well and mix thoroughly.
8. If you're using carrots, put them in the dish together with the dried apricots. Make sure to cover them with them with the juices.
9. Gently stir the ingredients. Mix everything well, but don't over mix it.
10. You can either use a crock pot or slow cooker. On high setting it will take approximately 3-4 hours or on automatic with keep warm facility up until 8 hours. Cooking times still depend on your crock pot.
11. If you're using a traditional tagine, slowly cook it with gas or over barbeque for 2-3 hours.
12. If doing with an electric tagine, process is the same as the slow cooker. Add corn flour mixed a little water to add some thickness.
13. Freshly chopped coriander or cilantro is a good garnish for this dish. Another would be serving it with couscous, rice, fresh flat bread, pita bread or salads. Pureed or mashed potatoes and pasta also go well along with this dish.

Nutrition Facts

Serving Size: 1 (546 g)
Servings Per Recipe: 6

Amount Per Serving	% Daily Value
Calories 488.7	
Calories from Fat 71	14%
Total Fat 7.9g	12%
Saturated Fat 1.3g	6%
Cholesterol 76.7mg	25%
Sugars 31.5 g	
Sodium 645.0mg	26%
Total Carbohydrate 71.7g	23%
Dietary Fiber 11.1g	44%
Sugars 31.5 g	126%
Protein 35.9g	71%

Variation: Cut up portions of chicken pieces or whole chicken is also a good alternative; but remember to fry them until brown before it goes to the dish. Preserved lemons are as well a wonderful addition to this. Add them together with the apricots and carrots.

Savory Cube Steak and Gravy

Prep Time: 15 mins

Total Time: 8 hrs 15 mins

Servings: 4

Ingredients
- 2 lbs cube steaks
- salt
- pepper
- flour (for dredging)
- 1 (1 ounce) package onion gravy mix
- 1 (10 1/2 ounce) cans cream of mushroom soup
- 2 cups water

Directions
1. Season the steaks with salt and pepper. Cover the steaks with flour.
2. In a skillet or frying pan, brown the steak and transfer to crock pot.
3. Pour the water, soup, and gravy mix.
4. Seal your crock pot. Cook on low setting for 6-8 hours.

5. Best to serve with mashed potatoes or rice.

Nutrition Facts

Serving Size: 1 (193 g)
Servings Per Recipe: 4

Amount Per Serving		% Daily Value
Calories 63.2		
Calories from Fat 39		62%
Total Fat 4.3g		6%
Saturated Fat 1.0g		5%
Cholesterol 0.0mg		0%
Sugars 1.0 g		
Sodium 525.9mg		21%
Total Carbohydrate 5.0g		1%
Dietary Fiber 0.0g		0%
Sugars 1.0 g		4%
Protein 1.2g		2%

Variation: You can add more gravy as much as you like. I like a lot!

Down Home Crock Pot Chili

Prep Time: 30 mins

Total Time: 6 hrs 30 mins

Servings: 4-6

Ingredients

Seasoning Mix
- 4 tablespoons chili powder
- 2 1/2 teaspoons ground coriander
- 2 1/2 teaspoons ground cumin
- 1 1/2 teaspoons garlic powder
- 1 teaspoon oregano
- 1/2 teaspoon cayenne pepper

Chili
- 1 1/2 lbs ground beef
- 1 tablespoon minced onion
- 1 (28 ounce) cans diced tomatoes
- 1 (15 ounce) cans tomato sauce
- 2 (15 ounce) cans kidney beans

Directions

1. In a small bowl, combine the seasoning mix.
2. Store the seasoning mix in an airtight container away from any moisture or too much heat. For this recipe, only 5 tsp would be used.
3. Cook ground beef in a skillet. Cook until the meat is no longer pink.
4. Drain the beef to remove excess oil.
5. Include the onion and 3 tsp of seasoning mix.
6. Add tomatoes, tomato sauce, one can of beans, and 2 more teaspoons of seasoning mix.
7. The other can of beans would go into the blender. Process it until it becomes smooth.
8. Remove the beans in the blender, and put it together with the meat in the crock pot.
9. Stir the recipe thoroughly.
10. Set the heat on low and cook for about 6-8 hours.

Nutrition Facts

Serving Size: 1 (468 g)
Servings Per Recipe: 4

Amount Per Serving		% Daily Value
Calories 642.3		
Calories from Fat 261		40%
Total Fat 29.0g		44%
Saturated Fat 10.6g		53%
Cholesterol 115.6mg		38%
Sugars 14.4 g		
Sodium 1447.7mg		60%
Total Carbohydrate 50.7g		16%
Dietary Fiber 18.9g		75%
Sugars 14.4 g		57%
Protein 47.5g		95%

Variation: You can remove the beans if they are not your thing or replace them with another kind of bean.

In Closing

I love to cook. I believe it brings together families and friends. So I hope you and your family enjoy the delicious slow cooker recipes in this book and remember to save a seat for me at the table!

Pamela

WANT MORE RECIPES?

Join my newsletter so that you get the first crack at all new cookbooks that are released! And as always, our members get them at a special discount!

Just go to **PJRECIPES.COM** and sign up. It's free!

Also don't forget to check out my other titles on Amazon.